What Happy Dogs Know

Glenn Dromgoole

SOURCEBOOKS, INC.®
NAPERVILLE, ILLINOIS

Published by Sourcebooks, Inc.
P.O. Box 4410, Naperville, Illinois 60567-4410
(630) 961-3900
FAX: (630) 961-2168
www.sourcebooks.com

ISBN 1-4022-0295-4

Printed and bound in China
SNP 10 9 8 7 6 5 4 3 2 1

For Sam and Ellen

The tricks dogs teach us.

The tricks dogs teach us are more important than any tricks we can ever teach them.

We teach them to beg, roll over, and fetch. They teach us about loyalty, friendship, enthusiasm, joy, patience, forgiveness, and unconditional love.

We teach them with words. They teach us with actions.

We teach them to be obedient. They teach us to be observant.

We teach them about the meaning of commands. They teach us about the meaning of life.

No whining.

Why do we complain so much? Isn't that one of the things we like about dogs? They never complain.

After dealing all day with criticisms, whines, and complaints everywhere we turn—from the boss, from fellow workers, from customers, from commuters—it's refreshing to come home and be greeted with happiness, acceptance, and an enthusiastic kiss.

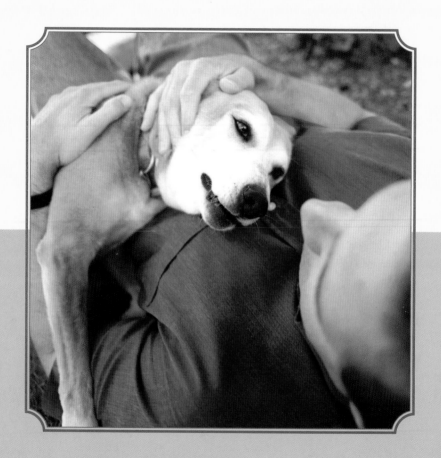

Just say thanks.

Dogs are so appreciative of even the slightest favor or attention—a pat on the head, a dog biscuit, a romp in the backyard.

We, on the other hand, rarely stop to say thanks.

If we said thank you as often and as sincerely as dogs do, we might find we like each other as much as we like our dogs. (We might even get more favors and attention, too.)

Get some fresh air.

We've become so spoiled by air-conditioning that we forget to roll down the car windows and enjoy the fresh air on a warm day.

Given a choice, a dog will pick fresh air nearly every time. And why not?

Everyone—whatever their pedigree— should get to experience the exhilarating thrill of riding around town in a convertible.

Shake hands.

One of the first tricks we teach our dogs is to shake hands. We should teach our kids to do so, too.

It's one of the basic tricks everyone should learn at an early age. Shake hands firmly, look the other person in the eye, smile, and speak up.

OK, Junior, now you may have a cookie.

Fetch the paper.

I haven't seen any surveys on this, but I suspect not as many dogs are taught to bring in the newspaper every morning as there used to be. Likely, it is because not as many of us read the paper, preferring to get our news from TV or the Internet.

But newspapers still provide both depth and breadth of coverage—especially news and information about local happenings—in a convenient, clip-able, time-saving, portable package that you can—um—sink your teeth into.

Here, boy, bring me the…no, not the remote, the paper!

Play together.

We spend a lot of money on high-tech toys—for children and for adults. Dogs remind us that we don't need expensive toys to entertain ourselves.

A Frisbee or a ball or stick will do just fine, providing you have someone else to play with.

It requires an investment of time and togetherness, not money.

Be content.

Dogs are not very demanding. All they ask is a little companionship, plenty of food, and an opportunity to go to the bathroom.

As our lives get more complicated, maybe we need to take notes from watching our dogs.

Relax a little more and enjoy each other's company. Be content with what we have. Take a nap. Eat a little. Take another nap.

Grrrrr.

When the doorbell rings at our house, the dogs start barking. I'm not sure if they can't wait to see who is there, or they just wish we could be left alone.

I have the same conflicting feelings when the telephone rings. Don't you feel like barking when your dinner is interrupted by a telemarketing call? Before giving in to that urge, however, we might stop to consider that the person on the other end of the line has probably been barked at all day long.

So much for growling.

Lest we think we're more civilized than dogs when it comes to snarling and growling at each other, tune in to one of those trash-talk TV programs or professional wrestling or a daily newscast or a political campaign.

What are we so mad about?

Someone to confide in.

Who would you rather tell a secret to—your dog or your best friend?

We humans could be better confidants to each other if we would take a tip from our dogs. Listen more and talk less.

No rude behavior.

Thank goodness we don't all go around sniffing each other's crotches (except in singles bars).

Of course, we do go around sniffing out the latest rumor or gossip about somebody else.

We do go around butting into each other's business.

We do go around making inappropriate comments.

We do go around being insensitive to other people's feelings.

Treated like a dog?

Around our house, being treated like a dog is considered an elevation in status.

The dogs are waited on hand and foot. They don't have much to do except sleep and guard the property against intruding cats and squirrels.

We should have it so good.

On the other hand, that would probably get boring pretty quickly. We need challenges to feel alive.

You won't
miss much.

Dogs have the good sense to sleep through dull speeches and most of what's on television.

A campus bulldog at the college I attended would waddle into economics class, find a comfortable place to plop down, and promptly go to sleep.

Just like the rest of us.

Straining at the leash.

When I take my dogs for a walk, it's a challenge to keep them both going the same direction.

One of them always has to walk on the left. The other always has to be charging ahead out front. They don't seem inclined to compromise or accommodate each other's leanings...

...like some people we know.

Name tags.

In most cities, dogs are required to wear collar tags for public health reasons and to help locate lost pets.

I consider it a public service when *people* wear name tags as well, particularly at business and social functions. Maybe not for public health reasons, but for the mental health of those of us with an impaired capacity for remembering names.

Simple values.

Everyone ought to see a good dog movie every once in a while. And read a good dog book, of course.

Dog movies and dog stories remind us of the simple values we cherish in our lives and the emotional investment required for successful relationships.

Second chances.

One of the most famous dogs of all time was the movie dog Benji. Benji is a testimony to the power of grace in our lives.

Doomed to death in an animal shelter, Benji—or Higgins, as he was called then—was rescued by a Hollywood animal trainer and put to work, first on TV and then as a movie superstar.

Most of us don't have stories as dramatic as Benji's, but we can relate to being given a second or third chance to make something of ourselves.

A nose for news.

An old editor told me that a good journalist should be able to walk down the street and come back with enough news to fill the newspaper.

That's what dogs do when they go on a walk.

They have an innate curiosity, a "nose for news" that allows them to sniff out— on trees, tires, posts, hydrants—the who, what, when, and where of other dogs who have been on the trail before them.

It takes all kinds.

Watch a dog show sometime and appreciate the diversity represented there. Appreciate diversity not just in dogs, but in all of nature.

It not only would be dull if we were all alike, but impractical.

We have different interests, tastes, abilities, and strengths. Diversity is nature's way of making everything work.

The old dog.

You have to appreciate the faithfulness and courage of an old dog.

For years, the dog has been loyal to the family, always there for them, watching the kids grow up and go off to start their own families, welcoming them when they come home to visit.

Now, in the advanced years, the old dog suffers from a variety of ailments, but doesn't complain, and continues to keep the best interests of the family at heart.

An old dog is to be treasured, appreciated, respected, and loved.

Too much of a good thing.

Friendliness is an attribute to be admired in dogs and in people. But friendliness can be carried to an extreme.

Not everyone appreciates being jumped on when they enter a room—whether by a well-meaning dog or by an overzealous glad-hander.

A little restraint tends to always be appropriate.

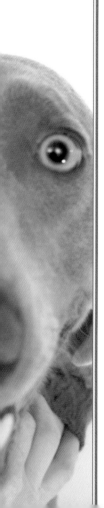

Just be there.

Dogs offer great comfort to elderly people.

An Alzheimer's patient, my dad always had his spirits lifted when his dog Bitsy would come to visit him in the nursing home.

Perhaps dogs sense, in a way that some of us can't, that they are needed to just be there and offer quiet, steady, loving companionship.

Mutts are us.

We can't all have a great pedigree, but we can be happy with who we are. Some of the best-loved dogs in the world are mutts.

Happiness doesn't depend on our status in life, but in feeling that we belong.

Listen.

Dogs have an acute sense of hearing. They can hear sounds that we humans can't.

For most of us, however, the problem is not so much that we can't hear as that we don't listen attentively to what we can hear. Tune in today.

A few points.

Leaders in business or other organizations can take a few pointers from bird dogs.

- To be successful, a team has to learn to work together.
- Always back each other up.
- Treat others right and they will train harder and work harder for you.
- Stay focused on the task at hand.
- Give credit when it is deserved.
- Don't point out the shortcomings of others.
- Be generous with praise and rewards.

Going in circles.

Like a dog trying to catch its own tail, we can find ourselves running around in circles going nowhere.

We wear ourselves out in pursuit of elusive goals or meaningless activities instead of putting our time and effort to work on more productive endeavors.

Dream big.

According to research, little dogs dream more than big dogs, young dogs more than old dogs. Of course, no one knows exactly what they dream about, because they can't tell us.

However, we do know what *we* dream of doing and what our children dream for themselves—even if they can't always articulate it—and those are dreams we should nurture and act on.

Pay attention to details.

Like fleas, little things can become a big problem if not dealt with early on. They pile up and the next thing you know, you feel out of control (or worse, you need a bath).

We should pay attention to those details—always keeping our objectives in mind, of course.

It gets all over us.

One of my dogs has a tendency to roll around in horse poop. I don't know why, and it's certainly not an endearing characteristic.

It gets all over her and really stinks up the place and no one wants to be around her—not unlike what happens to us when we wallow in self-pity and negativism.

Sing. Dance.

Every so often you see a dog on TV or somewhere who can sing or dance. Not very well, in fact, but that's just the point.

When it comes to singing and dancing, we don't have to have an abundance of talent or years of training to get a lot of satisfaction from it.

Sing. Dance. Celebrate.

Getting to know you.

As a boy, I developed a fear of dogs because a couple of them used to chase me on my bicycle. It didn't occur to me then that they probably just wanted to play.

Later, as I got to know a few dogs personally, I not only overcame my fear and prejudice toward dogs, but actually became quite a friend and advocate.

We shouldn't let our fears blind us to opportunities to get to know others.

No one's perfect.

Anyone who has lived with dogs very long can testify that dogs are certainly not perfect.

They eat furniture and other esteemed objects. They don't always make it outside before relieving themselves. They bark when everyone's trying to sleep. They shed. They jump on people, sometimes intimidate them, even hurt them.

The point is that even in their imperfection dogs have something to teach us about the meaning of life. For who among us can claim to be perfect? The best we can hope for is a measure of understanding and forgiveness and grace when we do what we shouldn't.

Soul connections.

Theologians may debate the question of whether dogs have souls and, if so, what their fate might be in the hereafter.

But for those of us who have been touched by the affection and loyalty and love of a dog, we know that truly their souls have connected with ours for whatever eternity we can comprehend.

Unrestrained joy.

When I come home after being away from the house for a while, the dogs get so excited that they go outside and run around and around the backyard. I call it "running the bases," and I take it as an expression of unrestrained joy that they are glad to see me.

Rarely are we greeted so enthusiastically by any of our human acquaintances.

No wonder dogs have a special place in our hearts.

Friendliness.

Friendliness, not cleanliness, is next to godliness. We'll take a dirty friend over a clean enemy anytime.

Of course, it's nice when the dirty friend takes a bath, brushes his teeth, and otherwise becomes presentable. Cleanliness is definitely a virtue, just not the predominant one.

Nap time.

Given a choice of lying on the couch or getting up and doing something productive, dogs are a lot like us—or we're a lot like our dogs.

And sometimes that's the right choice.

Saturday afternoons, for example, are good times for doing nothing but lying on the couch and watching a ball game or taking a nap—or both.

Buried treasure.

I'm waiting for the training program that teaches dogs to dig up crab grass. Dogs are good diggers, but wouldn't it be helpful if they dug up weeds instead of flowers?

On a deeper level, I suppose there are meaningful lessons to be learned from dogs' digging habits: if you want something, you have to dig for it. Or, we ought to bury a few bones for when we need them.

Sick as a dog.

The only time I've had to leave a dog in the hospital overnight was one time when I let her participate in a birthday celebration—that included chocolate cake.

Now, everyone knows that dogs shouldn't eat chocolate, right? As a novice dog person, I didn't. What I learned from that experience— besides not ever giving a dog chocolate—was:

a) ignorance is *not* bliss;
b) just because we want it doesn't mean we should have it; and
c) when you're very sick, go to the hospital.

Stop the game.

If a dog gets loose on the playing field of a ball game—it doesn't matter what sport: football, baseball, soccer, or yes, even basketball—what happens?

   a) Play stops while the participants try to get the dog off the field.
   b) The crowd loves it.

There's a lesson to be learned, which is that, above all, sports should be fun and not taken too seriously.

Smile.

Some dogs actually smile, or at least appear to be smiling. Many dogs laugh with their tails. Whatever the form, there's no denying that dogs can communicate their happiness.

So can we, though too often we don't.

Smile more. Laugh more. Celebrate the joy of being alive. Communicate that joy to others.

Merit badge.

Boy Scouts learn to be trustworthy, loyal, helpful, friendly, courteous, kind, obedient, cheerful, thrifty, brave, clean, and reverent.

Most of those virtues could be learned by earning a merit badge in dog care.

Yes, even "clean," "thrifty," and "reverent," when you think about it:

- most dogs bathe themselves;
- they don't have expensive habits or requirements; and
- they have a certain reverence, or respect, toward all of God's creatures.

Like, bark.

Should you, like, think that dogs are, like, inarticulate, you obviously haven't, like, talked to a teenager, like, lately.

To a dog, the word "like" has a specific meaning, as in, "Would you like a cookie?" or "Would you like to go outside?" or "I would like a kiss."

To a teenager, the word "like" isn't even a word; it's just, like, a grunt or a, like, pause for reassurance.

Dogs don't, like, bark; they just bark.

Simple thrills.

All I have to do is say the word "walk" or the phrase "a ride in the car" and the dogs launch into a frenzy of anticipation. For them, the simple thrills are still thrills.

These days we're so blasé, given all the amusement options available to us, that we don't get excited about very many things. We have lost our sense of wonder.

Dogs haven't.

Kids talk in questions?

When we are speaking to our dogs? We talk in questions, not in sentences? Like a lot of kids do? Like, there are no periods? Just question marks?

If dogs just nodded their heads when we were talking to them? They would probably be confused? Thinking we were asking a question when we were actually making a statement?

Blame the messenger.

Dogs have traditionally taken a special dislike to postal workers. People, on the other hand, tend to like the people who deliver the mail. We may not like everything we get in the mail, but we don't hold the carrier responsible. We certainly wouldn't think of biting him or her.

When it comes to news, however, aren't we often like our dogs—blaming the messenger for telling us things we would rather not hear or read about?

Don't worry
so much.

We assume that dogs worry. They seem to be especially fretful every time we leave, worrying that we won't be coming home to them.

But they don't appear to worry about money or about being popular or about what they're going to wear or about what the future holds.

Some people worry about whether they worry too much, or even whether they're too complacent and don't worry enough.

The lesson dogs teach us is that if we put our emphasis on relationships, we don't need to let ourselves get too worked up about everything else.

Too big of a hurry.

Most of us need to learn how to relax. If we have a spare minute, we spend it on the cell phone or computer figuring out how to make another buck, taking care of some last-minute detail, tending to a chore that needs to be done, or ferrying the kids off to still another lesson or event.

Our dogs, meanwhile, are lounging in the sun, admiring the beauty of a cloudless day. Or they're stretched out by the fireplace or under the air-conditioner wondering, perhaps, why everyone seems to be in such a hurry.

Profanity.

Do dogs cuss? I could swear that I've heard dogs cuss at me. At least their barking was so fierce I had to assume it wasn't just your common, everyday canine comment.

But if dogs do use profanity, I doubt that they use it as frequently or as indiscriminately as people do.

And dogs have an excuse for cussing—they don't have that large a vocabulary. We do—or should.

Good eating habits.

You occasionally see fat dogs, but not as often as you see fat people. Most dogs eat heartily a couple of times a day and don't snack in between. They drink a lot of water. They get plenty of sleep. They exercise.

If they get bored (and surely they must), they find ways to amuse themselves other than eating.

Enjoy the chase.

Dogs delight in chasing each other. I'm not sure they particularly want to catch each other—they simply enjoy the chase.

We are more likely to get satisfaction from our careers, our education, our families, and our hobbies if we don't become so obsessed with the end result that we forget to take pleasure from the process.

It's not how the game ends, it's how much we enjoy playing it. It's not making an A in a class that's most important, it's what we learn while pursuing the grade. It's not getting to our destination, it's what we see along the way.

A little humility.

The reason squirrels and cats can climb trees, and dogs can't, is because they are the "chasees" rather than the "chasers."

Nature made it that way to give the squirrels and cats some hope.

And also, perhaps, to teach dogs some humility. The one who barks the loudest doesn't always get his way.

A good walk.

A walk in the park,
A vigorous stroll.
It's good for the heart,
And great for the soul.

About the Author

Glenn Dromgoole is the author of ten books, including the best-selling *What Dogs Teach Us.* He is managing editor of State House Press and McWhiney Foundation Press, which publish books on Texas and Civil War history. His dogs, Pola and Honey, have been his inspiration.

Dog Credits